Out of the Dark:

One Person's Travels Through Grief

Out of the Dark:

One Person's Travels Through Grief

Poems by

Linda Whittenberg

Cover design by Shay Culligan
Cover image by deeonederer on Pexels
Author photo by Wendy Woods LLC

ISBN: 978-1-63980-732-1

Kelsay Books
502 South 1040 East, A-119
American Fork, Utah 84003
Kelsaybooks.com

We humans are a clan marked by matching scars. All of us eventually claim a place among those who grieve. It is my prayer that those who have known grief might find here words that resonate with their own experience and give some measure of comfort.

Acknowledgments

Poems in *Out of the Dark* previously appearing elsewhere:

Bristlecone Journal: "Start Anywhere"
Fixed and Free Poetry Anthology: "In Another Season"
Let Nothing Be Lost (Kelsay Books): "Soundings"
Trasna: "The Haunting Hat," "Start Anywhere," "Astronomical,"
    "Sangre de Cristos," "Visitation," "How Far Away Is Heaven?"
    (as "Since You've Been Gone")

In Gratitude

Always, members of the Santa Fe poetry group we call "The Praise Poets" have been my companions, giving me gentle critiques and just enough praise to keep me at it. Thank you: Jane Lipman, Blair Cooper, Jane Eigner, Georgia St. Clair, and John Hick.

I feel tremendous gratitude to those who listen to my newest work and share their honest reactions, especially Lucinda Duncan and Larry Saltzman.

Having just moved to a different state and grieving while the Covid epidemic raged would have been much worse had it not been for the online grief workshops offered by Marge Hahn.

I am particularly grateful to my long-time friend, Lynn Holm, who helped me with this book and has helped with every publication. Bless you, Dear Lynn.

Other Work by Linda Whittenberg

Dying Can Wait, Pudding House Press, 2009

Tender Harvest, Finalist for NM Book Award,
Black Swan Editions, 2009

Somewhere in Ireland, Black Swan Editions, 2011

Let Nothing Be Lost, Kelsay Books, 2014

Stone by Stone, Black Swan Editions, 2018

My Blue Heaven, published through Amazon, 2024

Contents

Inevitable	13
The Void	14
Sangre de Cristos	15
Astronomical	16
A Night at Yosemite	17
Wolf Country	19
Soundings	20
Remembering for Two	21
Visitation	22
You Have Become	23
All the Way to the End	24
Fathers and Sons	25
Homeward	27
Side by Side	28
Downpour	29
A Day Like This	30
With Half a Heart	32
The Lesser Gold Finches	33
Where I Live	34
Start Anywhere	35
The Haunting Hat	36
In Another Season	37
How Far Away Is Heaven?	38
The Way It Was	40
The Memorial	42
Found	44

Inevitable

It's built into the plan—loss.
How else would we discover
what we love most?

That Betsy-Wetsy doll made
of real rubber, a WWII treasure,
melted in the attic one Illinois summer.

It wasn't death, but seemed symbolic
since those years soldiers were dropping
halfway round the world.

Leaving, departing, disappearing,
that's life. Even forgetting
is a kind of dying.

Try to live without loss, go ahead,
make it your life's work—for it is.
That's our place in the world,

to hold back the flood, build a dike.
Even as hair falls out, teeth rot, we
begrudgingly admit there's no stopping it.

We put on a wig and contra dance
down at the Odd Fellows Hall, pretending
we don't know nothing lasts.

The Void

Your insides hollow as a sun-dried gourd.
Doggedly you try to fill the empty space.
Both the ordinary and the outrageous fail.
Absence plays background music through the day.

Doggedly you try to fill the empty space.
The escalator keeps moving toward forever.
Both the ordinary and the outrageous fail.
Sunset sprays vermilion across dry grasses.

The escalator keeps moving toward forever.
Candles burn down at the altar.
Sunset sprays vermilion across dry grasses.
You breathe in, breathe out, like everything alive.

Candles burn down at the altar.
A dangling strand leads out of the dark.
You breathe in, breathe out, like everything alive.
You discover longing can be a guide.

A dangling strand leads out of the dark.
The ordinary and the outrageous fail.
You discover longing can be a guide
Out of the dark.

Sangre de Cristos

Tender perennial sprouts appear, the clematis buds,
apricot leaves uncoil, overhead, migrating birds.
I fill the feeder.

My heart beats faster this time of year, plans form,
summer stretches ahead like Route 66 promising
a ride in a convertible.

It is an especially fine spring day when you return
from the doctor and plunk down a packet of papers
in the middle of the round oak kitchen table.

The lion paws on that table want to run. This table
where children formed awkward letters
on yellow, blue-lined pads. Oatmeal every morning.

That blue packet stared me down, the way two people play
who blinks first. Dr. Jackson came in the room that first day
saying, *At last, a normal-sized person,* for he too was very tall.

Today, he must have stuttered through what had to be said.
Did he look directly at you with the news? The results
must have broken poor Dr. Jackson's heart.

I read, but the letters swarm like bees, making it hard
to take in. Why is it always spring when bad news strikes?
Have we not had enough of loss?

Let's go outside together at sunset, My Love.
It's the kind of day when the sun going down will
most surely turn the mountains blood-red.

Astronomical

Amid tumult, when sleep
is hard to secure, I wake
to step out on flagstone and study
the sky which greets me
with a crescent moon hovering close
to a morning star, a pair so brilliant
and full of hope for a few seconds
I almost forget all I am losing,
even allow a flash of delight.
Two astronomical wonders cuddling
so close they appear inseparable,
but I am not dissuaded from my grief,
for I know days ahead a different sky
will display another vision of reality—
a lone star, probably faithful Venus,
less illuminating, yet, still shining,
still doing its part to light up the sky.

A Night at Yosemite

Those tents on platforms, Curry Village,
that's where we slept one cold night
below Half Dome and the falls.

We were not yet under each other's skin
or wedded in any way, but newly discovering
what this mad attraction was to be.

Cold, I can't find words, for how cold
it was, and I was not well, coming down
with something that gave me shivers

and a fever, so we shared one of the twin beds,
piled on strata of covers. That's when
you kept my mind off my misery

by telling army stories of Germany
in the late '50s, peacetime military,
nothing grim or bloody,

only funny—how you were assigned
to the library where you read many books
as service to your country.

Weekends you flew to any place army airfreight
planes were going, thus seeing most of Europe.
How it was, when one of your comrades

who was always late for curfew, came in late again,
He'd asked his comrades to cover too many times,
and so, you threw his cot out the barracks window.

Christmas in Nuremberg, stumbling down
dry canals, arm in arm, slurring carols
at the top of your inebriated lungs.

It was nearly morning when I finally fell asleep,
your body next to mine, having crossed some zone
from hesitation to surrender and the war was won.

Wolf Country

You and I climb a hill to wait as light
lazily sweeps down the valley,
adorning spidery trees, frost-covered grasses
in shades of gold. There's urgency in the air
with winter at the door. Geese overhead make
anxious noise. We pray to see wolves.

Today, the Druid pack is on the prowl.
Look there, you call out, *Along the ridge!*
We both focus binoculars, awestruck.
We make out five, two black, three grays.
The intensity of hunger is evident in their focus,
their stride. Tears come, I've waited so long
for this thrill.

Few words pass between us. We're wrapped
in what it took for this day of wolf justice
to come, this marvel of healthy wolves,
free at last, to roam. We recall how often
we've said we could not die without seeing
wolves in the wild.

Soundings

*... the signals we give—yes or no, or maybe—
should be clear: the darkness around us is deep.*
—William Stafford, "A Ritual to Read to Each Other"

Your *yes,* really a *no* that fears displeasing.
I slather irritations with whipped cream.
Some days we let pettiness drive the car
while we dispute the best way to Agua Fria.

When it turns out you are right—again,
I vow to quit quibbling.
The trouble with words is once they're out there
making fools of themselves, they can't be caned in.

That's why I want you to know—
when your hearing aids malfunction
or when I misconstrue your meaning,
I think of it as ambient noise and of us
as two blue whales whose songs vibrate
down where the sea is dark and deepest.

Remembering for Two

I used to consider how it would be
if the worst were to come. Suppose
our memories were to crack and shatter
until only shards remained buried
under layers of sunbaked sand?
What would become of the *us* we have been?

Would I forget your eyes, so like the pool
under the waterfall, so sparkling and deep?
What if my memory should one day need
to remember Grass Mountain for both of us,
the purest kind of joy we both felt riding through
the green fescue, chest deep on our mules?

Or only one of us could tell how it was that time,
tent walls heavy with hail, ice forming on canvas,
supper out of a shared can, only each other's
body heat to keep warm.

And what of bedtime poems? the one with the rock
that speaks only once in a lifetime? And songs,
Hello, old friend, hello, isn't that how it goes?

Visitation

This morning, when went out to meet
the sunrise, a lone Whooping Crane
entered my mind. It might have been
the very one that surprised me once
at Bosque del Apache Bird Sanctuary.

There it was, in my imagining,
knee-deep at the edge of the pond,
just as I had witnessed it, so rare
that to see one felt like a blessing.

This morning that bird came
with the first light that feeds my soul—
soft rays of violet and delegate rose
spread over flowers and the wicker rocker
on the porch.

I felt that crane wanted to be remembered,
wanted me to put its elegant body
here to be eulogized as one who flew far—
long wings, long neck, haunting call,

one who,
like the one who used to rock
in that wicker chair, is gone
or nearly gone forever
except in this poem.

You Have Become

When dawn brings me joy as it always has,
I wonder how that can be. Only yesterday,
it seems, we worked to get you up
from the leather chair, practiced until
the weight was no problem at all, like dancing
to Country Western tunes.

I must admit lately my mind seesaws.
Memories undulate like heat waves
on hot pavement though it is winter. That circle
of aspen where you rest is covered in snow,
but the meadow open to sunlight is perfect
for the aster seeds mixed with ash.

In autumn I will go there to see if they bloom,
lie down in the warm sun to nap, the way
we always did after a long climb. I'll bring
the dogs.

Your little notebooks filled with tremorous script
I keep in the drawer of my desk. Some are lists
of things accomplished, crossed off. Most
I can't make out, but it feels as if there is something

you want me to get from the store or maybe
the lists were just for you, a reckoning
of things you intended to finish before
it was too late.

As I think back to that last smile, the way
your eyes shone with light I thought
was for me, now I wonder if it was, instead,
something else you saw, a new dawn.

All the Way to the End

I would have wished for you better lungs,
like Louis Armstrong blowing his horn,
cheeks ballooned. On the other hand,
I was no Brunhilda where climbing
was concerned, and besides we enjoyed
our rests along upward trails of the Valhalla,

naps on Grass Meadow while our mules
grazed in bliss, and then, there was
that time at Glacier, when we woke
to the roar of a Grizzly which turned out to be,
instead, the whir of a hummingbird.

We wrote our own fairy tale,
with remarkable twists and turns.
You used to say—*Take life as it comes,*
but do your best to make it come
as you would like it.
A good guide toward happiness, I learned.

Together we lived a good story, didn't we?
All the dance moves we mastered, becoming
mule crazy together, numerous trips to Ireland,
seven within ten years, a tribute to the simple
surprise of being alive and together.

I give thanks to whatever led me that night
to ask you to dance. On many strolls
through Manitou Park, we sat on our favorite
iron bench to watch the swan pair glide.
Now I am paddling as best I can, a lone duckling.
You have become the swan.

Fathers and Sons

What is it sons want from
their fathers? Fatherhood must be
a stack of silver coins paid
out in fishing lines, shot gun
shells, billiard balls, slaps
on the back.

Or there must
be some secret words
to utter at the right time,
in the right tone of voice.
Since I never had a father
and was a girlchild,
I try to understand
that currency because,
now that he's gone

I'd like to treat their wounds
with words, my currency,
but they fail. Instead, I make
cranberry salad, their holiday
favorite, give them parts
of him to keep—
the antelope watercolor
that is so fine, the framed quote
from Kennedy, declaring
the honor of government work,
all his desk could hold
of mementoes

baby pictures,
high school report cards,
certificates of their births.
I made sure one of them got
the leather gloves shaped
to his hand.

Homeward

From the patio, traffic sounds
seem more evident than when you sat
in the Amish rocker watching birds
at the feeder and I sat nearby, as we
chatted about upcoming elections
or how the garden was doing.

Now, alone at night, if I leave
the window open, even a crack,
I hear that traffic whir
like Om sounded by a hundred
kneeling monks broadcasting,
Life goes on.

Emptiness is filled with motors
and wheels—motorcycle roar,
blown out mufflers, throaty rumble
of trucks, an occasional drag race,
wail of siren's intent on rescue or arrest.

Worst is at 5 PM, workers, homebound.
An extraordinary word, *homebound.*
It makes my throat quiver as I say it.
I always called out to you, as I came
in the door—
I'm home, Sweetheart, I'm home.

Side by Side

Last night, when a full moon crept over the foothills,
you called me to the window so we could stand
side by side to take in the wonder,

the way we stood by the ponds of the Bosque,
tremor of a thousand cranes vibrating in our chests,
the way, after an arduous climb, we stood breathless
on a ledge to take in miles of Utah's sandstone sculpture,

the way we stood on the west coast of Ireland
bracing ourselves against the wild winds of the Atlantic,
the way, at dawn in the tropics, we stood on the roof
of a Mayan ruin to watch birds and monkeys dart and swing
through treetops,

the way we always stand side by side to wave as our children
and their children pull out of the driveway, the way we did,
coming down the aisle side by side to make promises
we have kept all these years.

The way, I know, one day, there will be only one of us
standing, and then, when the moon comes over the foothills
just after sunset, the one left will see that silver light
as if it were for two.

Downpour

The most wondrous memories
of my life have no proof in photos.
It seems I might have made them up,
but then, how could they be so vivid?

That night, when we were newlyweds
and left the dishes after dinner to take a walk
as the summer evening was descending.

The first sprinkles of rain we scarcely noticed,
occupied as we were with each other,
learning first lessons in what this conjoining
would deliver.

Then, drops getting bigger, then the downpour,
our thin summer clothes drenched, sticking
to us.

The scramble back to comfort of the home
you had brought me to as bride,
not young, but young enough to take in
the pleasure of new love.

The giggling joy of it.
We were old enough to know
the value of what we had.

A Day Like This

Chances are you've had a day
like this, one stretching out
with nothing in it,
four walls that mock
your emptiness, that longing
for anyone at all who could
break the quiet, derision
that you can't do better,
chiding that you've let
yourself get in this state
of grief, immobilized by dread
that keeps you from the phone
on the dresser, front door
that connects to a sidewalk,
practically new Honda, keys
hanging on a hook that leads
to the garage, the computer
shut down, modem
dropped connection, not
a creative word in you,
not even bad poetry,
as your mind flips through
memories, days when you
were not alone, a file of names,
people you call friends,
neighbors, family, names that say
they love you and you know
you love them,
all those good times,
squeezed in
around your dinner table,
always strays who had

nowhere else to go,
times people said,
Oh, I wish
you could stay longer,
even times people
called on you
because they were distraught,
alone, afraid, even desperate,
but it's Sunday,
everyone has plans,
and you would hate
knowing you'd interfered
or worse, they felt pity,
sad for your grieving,
but now all that blurs
behind a gauzy scrim
that separates you
from even your dogs
who look at you, longing
for a walk, the birds
at the feeder,
that still small voice
you've always heard,
the one that says,
You are a lover of life,
never forget it.

With Half a Heart

If I live with half a heart, time beats half as fast.
If time begins to crawl, water takes longer to boil.
If eggs take too long to hard boil, I lose appetite for breakfast.
If the newspaper no longer comes, the news is always bad,
For no one sits at the table by the window turning pages.

If I have half a heart even bird songs are half as beautiful.
If I wear long skirts to hide the limp, no one notices.
If the right hand is shriveled, I shake with the left.
If I'm very quiet, they won't notice I've moved to a foreign nation,
For I packed a valise in the night and half of me went.

If no one is there, how can I write home?
If the hole in my chest widens, it will be hard to conceal the
    wound.
If I don't take off my wedding ring, will I still be married?
If I turn up the volume, I won't hear my bones shrinking.
For I want to remember—shape of his face, his twinkling eyes.

If I try harder, maybe I can get to the other side of losing.
If I'm on the phone, they can't see how scarred I've become.
If I paint on a cheery face, they won't notice I'm fading,
If only I had enough epoxy to put things back together,
For I am beginning to crumble.

If this were a movie, I'd be good at dying.
If the food is tasty, no one notices the empty chair at the head of
    table.
If I am extra busy, it's because it's hard for one to live for two.
If I write this crazy poem, you'll know I'm grieving.
For I can't sleep in a bed half empty, half-heart scarcely beating.

If I feel like dying, don't worry, something holds me here.
For, if this is the price for loving, I'd do it all again.

The Lesser Gold Finches

From the sunroom window, we admire
flashes of gold, brightest plumage
found here in the high-desert, and,
for that, appreciated even more.

Small pleasures help us forget climate
disasters, places where wars and riots
clamor, the relentless ache behind the news.
These birds claim our attention absolutely.

We are honored that finch,
like the mated pairs that spread their wings,
bright yellow under-wings revealed. honor us
by choosing our millet, our seeds of sunflower.

We think that could be us, dancing in air,
fluttering to the same music,
all the while, knowing, when one of us
is ready to fly away, the other cannot follow.

Where I Live

I live between your BLM belt buckle
and the Dyson vacuum cleaner, between
green chili stew and gray oatmeal,
between the silk shirt I gave you
at Christmas and yoga pants.
This in-between has a ping-pong champ
at each end of the table.

Between your ashes
spread in an aspen grove
and the mystery novel
that puts me to sleep.
In my dreams the mules are still
waiting in the paddock to be fed
while I watch tv eating chocolates
that are making me fat.

Mornings, I live folded between
snapping pages of the newspaper,
between bad news and obituaries
where we find out who's died.
I live between your cowboy hats
and dances at the brewery just down
the road.

Between riding horseback
through golden quake of autumn
and getting the trash out; between
our place on Rabbit Run and the little house
on Miller; a thousand cranes
rising at dawn and your aged Heeler
who follows me from room to room.
She knows better than anyone
what I've lost.

Start Anywhere

Take the garage—
piles for Goodwill: backpacks
up and down mountains
for forty years,
tents where our co-mingled breath
beaded on the interior,
all kinds of gadgets
for repairing, installing, maintaining.

Chances are good,
no matter where I start,
the toolbox will get you even more
than the closet or dresser or desk.
Maybe it is because objects there
hold remains of his sweat.

The clawhammer handle still carries
traces of where he gripped it building a ramada
toward the back of the yard, a high place
for the best view of the moon rising
over the mountains on cool summer nights.

Start anywhere and you'll come
to the ramada, happy days wrestling logs,
a swing placed just right for moongazing.
Many nights we sat, arms intwined,
waiting for that luminescent sphere to peak
over the crest, dogs at our feet, mules
and even an exceptional goat in the paddock.
Start anywhere and you'll come to this—
glories of love lived here.

The Haunting Hat

Your cowboy hat still sits as you left it
on the hall closet shelf, chin strap tied up
to shape the brim. I reach for a scarf—
there you are.

Knowing I liked that hat,
you always wore it to the airport
when you came to pick me up.
There you were—
my handsome cowboy, waiting
to welcome me home.

The boots I gave to Goodwill, journals
fit nicely in a drawer, wedding ring made
by our Navajo friend resides in my jewelry box.

But the question gnaws—
how long do I keep the cowboy hat
with your sweat in the band?

In Another Season

In the garden, last year's perennials
were only stalks, dried seed heads,
shriveled leaves; yet, this spring,
up from the earth came green.

I have said, I will be okay.
Not hubris, a boast, rather a prediction
based on experience of knowing myself.

Confidence comes from the many times
I've chosen yes over no. As it was,
years ago, when I packed the red Subaru
and headed west alone.

It comes too from having danced
with death many times, burying
loved family one by one,
most often in spring when lilacs bloom.

I'm not saying it won't be hard,
not saying no self-doubt, fear, loneliness.
There will be grief, my body and soul
will mourn, but—

like the black foot daisies, that scatter
their seeds in a new place every spring,
I will find a way to bloom.

How Far Away Is Heaven?

Remember watching the insect-sized bicyclist
cross the vast terrain below the mesa?
Remember how strange it was to realize
that little dot was moving?
Then we were captivated by thoughts of the rider,
his thighs aching, heavy breathing, as he became.
not merely a dot in the desert, but human.
Maybe that's how it is.

I must look closely, for all that was you
could not have disappeared completely.
You were large, a real cowboy in your hat
and boots; and when you were on horseback
you were grand. The care you took
with your grooming, ironed shirts, crease
in jeans, you were a person who made
the most of living.

That's why I set aside reason and look
closely not to miss a sign, a hint,
a keyhole glimpse of you. There are times
when I reach out for you in my restless stirring
and find you there for the second before
the empty pillow.

It's something like wondering where the rose
goes in winter. How I fret, thinking perhaps
my favorites will not make it; and then, one
day, I am surprised by the first budding. That's
the way my imagination works—you are not gone,
merely dormant.

I will go to the mountain in late summer to see
if the asters we mixed with your ashes have
made it into flowering. I don't know
how far away heaven is or if there even is one,
but I keep looking.

The Way It Was

It had taken years, but we had
our theologies sorted out.
Far from the god handed down to us,
we had chiseled out a faith we could
live by—a way of seeing that
made sense, a compass we followed
to find our way.

For us poetry was closer to scripture
or any sacred text had been.
After dinner, we stayed long
at the table reading favorites aloud,
and many nights

one of us fell asleep
to the other's voice reading
beautiful words.

Little did we know,
lurking around corners of our house,
was a shadowy form with a plan
for us. Everything we'd learned,
the good living we had done,
even our love was put to the test.

We grieved losses but were saved
from bitterness, for we had come
to revere the world just as it is.
Birth to death, the cycle
every living thing passes through,
and why should we be different?

You were grateful for the time
you'd been given, and we both
for the miracle that, out of all
the people on earth, we had
met at all.

The Memorial

It was during Covid so only thirty could
attend, but I know you would have liked
the intimacy of it. The day, one of those
gorgeous September days New Mexico
gives us, sky blue, trees beginning to turn,
Chamisa, golden along the wall. Location,
the churchyard with the ancient apricot tree,
pride of the congregation, as back drop.

All this, so perfect, but, when I got up
to deliver the eulogy something felt wrong—
you were not there in the third row
smiling up at me with the look I'd come
to count on, one that said, *Say it,*
My Dearest Wife, tell them
what you know!

All those Sundays, the church service
never started until you were present.
I always knew I could look out and calibrate
the service by the vibes you gave off while I was
delivering words you'd heard
and helped polish the night before.

If it's possible for those who've passed on
to see through some veil, I believe you
would have enjoyed your memorial.
I remember, when I was gathering
the music, all your favorites, inviting
the musicians, mostly neighbors and friends,
preparing my remarks, all of it was measured
by what I knew would meet your approval.

And that day, since you were not there,
I had to imagine you giving me
one of those smiles that meant,
My love, you did okay.

Found

Car key fobs, some never found, and it costs plenty
to replace them; my purse is always hiding;
glasses, I finally bought two pair and somedays
can't find either; passwords rise into the ether.
I have spent a good deal of my precious later years
as a huntress.

The Rolodex in my brain loses names of people
I've known for years; favorite movies I can never
see again because I forgot the title!
Names of historical figures I know so well
they could be family, gone. Names,
lose them and the world begins to fog over.

Losing, you learn, is built into everything.
You lose those so close to your heart you think
you'll die—all your kin, those whose veins
pumped the same blood, even your truest love.
Giants, heroes who propped up your world,
killed off by bullets, old age or cruel illness.

Your rivers shrink, creeks dry up, mountains lose
their glaciers, blue skies sag gray with pollution.
Losing is so natural you wake up every morning
to find out what else has vanished—birds, jungles
and rain forests, entire tribes of people, their languages,
their knowledge.

But this is a poem about finding. You are surprised
by a spectacular sunrise, even better than all
the others that made you gasp.

Each day new delights—
empanadas, right in your city; bread with cranberries
and walnuts baked in; every year a new pop star
just when Neil Diamond has faded, Tony Bennet
is gone, and Willie is getting even more grizzled.

Sometimes you find what you had given up
on finding or didn't allow yourself to wish for,
as surprising as coming on a giant redwood
in your front yard or an eagle landing
on the porch. Sometimes you must go out
the front door, pick up the phone to find,
for instance, a best friend, almost a sister,
just when you had nearly settled on becoming
a lonely old lady.

And, okay, here's the rest—found, a sweetheart
who knew how loss can rob your happiness,
someone who was also looking for friendship
and even love. Don't tell me all is lost, ask me
and I'll prove it—finding is the lining sewn
into losing.

About the Author

Linda Whittenberg's poems find their roots in Illinois black loam but spread to both coasts and across the ocean to Ireland, where she has traveled many times to study poetry and explore the land of her ancestry.

Writing in the early hours each day has resulted in the publication of six volumes of poems. Her work has been published widely in journals and anthologies, most notably in *Rattle, Spoon River Review,* and *Revival,* an Irish publication.

After retiring from Unitarian Universalist ministry, she returned to Santa Fe with her husband, Bob Wilber. There she became an avid quilter and horsewoman. After her husband's death in 2021, she moved to the Denver Area to be nearer to three grown children and their families.

www.ingramcontent.com/pod-product-compliance
Lightning Source LLC
Chambersburg PA
CBHW031008090426
42737CB00008B/729